Darkness Unchained

Amanda Smith

BookLeaf Publishing

India | USA | UK

Presentation by *BookLeaf Publishing*

Web: www.bookleafpub.com

E-mail: info@bookleafpub.com

ISBN: 9789357447515

First edition 2022

DEDICATION

To Keith, Brittany, Megan, Nicole and Kathleen. Thank you for your support and encouragement.

ACKNOWLEDGEMENT

I would like to thank those who have supported and encouraged me to keep writing.
My biggest supporters are my husband Keith Smith, my best friend Brittany Allary who I'd spend most of my time with in high school writing stories and sharing ideas; my sister Nicole Heiser who would spend her free time writing with me, my other sister Megan Kessler who helped by reviewing my poetry and my mom Kathleen Burns who has always said I could do whatever I put my mind too.

PREFACE

Most of the poems in Darkness unchained are
my struggles as a teen and coping with the
events life has thrown my way. My poems are
also about my journey into my spirituality and
beliefs.
Writing has always been an outlet for me and the
emotions I was unsure of how to process.

Unexpected

Lurking in the trees
Is an enemy worse than death
Watching you from the shadows
Your every Step

Swimming in the waters
Are beasts long forgotten
Waiting for their prey
Given by their master

Walking down the road
Are everyday people
Unknown to the danger
That you're forever hunted

Hiding in the shadows
Is your past and regrets
Reaching up to snatch you
And make you its prisoner

Invisible around you
Are the guards of your soul
Protecting you from enemies
so, you can change the world

Love, Life and Lies

Where many fields have died
And sorrows long burdened
Lives a truth no one can deny
Of love, life and lies

Where many people have died
And pain was long suffered
Lies a truth no one can bare
Of love, life and lies

Where many animals have died
And entire existences wiped out
Lies a truth no one can deny
Of love, life and lies

Where many feelings have survived
Pain and loss remembered
Lies a truth no one can hear
Of love, life and lies

Everyone pays

The darkest of nights
The darkest of days
Everyone pays
Everyone pays

A vacant dark lot
A vacant destroyed town
We're all done now
All done now

A deserted house
An abandoned home
Here people roam
Dead people roam

A full cemetery
With cracking headstones
Where no one mourns
No one mourns

A large bed
A man with a hole in his head
The bad mans dead
Bad mans dead

A dying woman
with no reason to go on
Takes the shot bought
The shot bought

A city of death
A city of ghosts
There's no one left now
No one left now

Sacred Winds

The sacred winds are stirring
Something in darkness is luring
It's quick when it strikes
Places the heads on pikes
And eyes are forever staring

No freedom for their souls
They are mindless like trolls
They are the devil's new hand
Forever watching this land
Forced to do his bidding

They are chosen by Satan
But he is also mistaken
For he gives them no choice
All they need is a leader

Someone who can win
And knows what has been
They've been looking for so long
They know they can't go wrong
For if they do, he awakens

The army is coming
And they are doing there summing

To find out if they can win
Or pain awaits their loved ones and kin
They must have their way

Blood and gore are the plan
To conquer the evil plan
The only way to victory
Is that of clever trickery
If that indeed is the case

Are they so wise?
Can they win this prize?
The circle of darkness is growing
We must act before it starts showing
We cannot let people know

If the war goes on
It must be a clever con
For if the people know
It will ruin the earthly flow
For the world can't change overnight

After it is over and done with
It will arise like an urban myth
Until people can accept
Things they do not percept
And they can make a choice

For what this is about

Is a person's doubt
About the judgement at hand
Falling through the sand
The judge will be judged again

If we stick to the plan
We can start a new clan
That'll make the world better
We need to find the ancient letter
To remind us of our humanity

The sacred winds are stirring
Our plans in darkness are luring
For if we win this fight
It can end here tonight
And everyone on earth is learning

Look into my eyes

Look into my eyes
Tell me what you see
Do you see the lies
Or the truth that lies beneath

Look into my eyes
Tell me what you feel
Do you feel the pain?
That to me is so real

Look into my eyes
Do you see the gold?
Do you see the stories?
That I haven't told

Look into my eyes
Do you see the fear?
The fear that I know
What is coming here

Look into my eyes
Do you feel the hate?
For those who don't understand
And judge my fate

Look into my eyes
Do you feel the sadness?
That I will never
Be fully complete

Look into my eyes
Can you see my past?
Or is it a blur
Due to my madness

Look into my eyes
Can you see my love?
Do you see the fate?
Given by the Gods above

Look into my eyes
Can you feel my soul?
Do you see who I am
And how I must grow

Look into my eyes
Can you see who I am
Or is your mind clouded
By your judgements

Look into my eyes
Can you look into my eyes?
Or are you afraid
Of what may lie inside

I dream of night

I dream of night
I dream of freedom
I dream of the impossible
I dream of immortality

To dream is not to hold
To be free is to be unchained
To believe is to be wise
To live forever one must die

I dream of power
I dream of strength
I dream of wisdom
I dream of fate

To have power is not having brains
To have strength makes you weak
To dream of wisdom makes you dumb
To dream of fate is to die

I dream of safety
I dream to live
I dream to love
I dream to exist

To be safe is to be in danger
To survive is not to live
To hate is not to love
To be is not to exist

I dream to hold
I dream to feel
I dream to care
I dream to see

To hold is to be held
To be is to love
To care is to be cared for
To see is to see the truth

I dream of senses
I dream of realization
I dream of hope
I dream to live

To sense is to miss details
To realize is not to sense
To hope is to be disappointed
To live is only to die

Come to the Goddess

Come to the waters of the Goddess
Look and see the truth
Find the path that long ago was lost
Look to the Gods and Goddesses for guidance
For they lead even the ones astray

Come to the fire of the Goddess
Look and see your passion
Find the love that long ago was lost
Look to the Goddess for guidance
For they've given love to those who don't care

Come to the air of the Goddess
Look and see your spirit fly
Find the wisdom of all the ages
Look to the Gods for guidance there
For even they give knowledge to the dumb

Come to the earth of the Goddess
See the footprints of the past
Find the pain left by others
Look to the divine to heal her cuts

For even they can't heal earths sickness

Look in yourself and find the Goddess
See the creator in you and me
Find your soul gift from above
Thank them by believing in them
For if you do, they'll live forever

The Creature

Lying inside my body
Is a creature you cannot see
Anger that hasn't been unleashed
Fear that hasn't been to be

Lying inside my mind
Is a creature that doesn't care
Pain no human can bear
Reality that soon turns to insanity

Lying inside my body
Is the power to kill the world
Fate soon acknowledged
By one little girl

Lying inside my mind
Is a labyrinth of locked doors,
Frustration an immense creature
That washes up on the shore

Lying inside my body
Is happiness I can't achieve
For as soon as I grasp it
It slips away from me

Lying inside my mind
Is a truth that is untold
For if the world knew
It would slowly unfold

Injuries of Life

Cuts and scars
Symbols of the pain
You have overcome in life
Obstacles you had to sidestep

Burns and Blood
Symbols Of what you've endured
To go forward
Things you've sacrificed to survive

Injuries and mind loss
Symbols of what you've hidden
So, you would not be judged
So, you could live again

Broken bones and stiches
Symbols of your Curiosity
While living in the world
And what You've learned on your own

Cuts and Scars
Symbols of how you survived
Burns and blood
Symbols of what you've done

Injuries and mind loss
Symbols of what life's done for you
Broken bones and stitches
Symbols of newfound knowledge

What the world needs

Open water
Open faith
What the world needs
Is a common grave

Burning fire
Burning passion
What the world needs
Is a little compassion

Sprinkling water
Spilling Tears
What the world needs
Is common Love

Breathing Fire
Breathing fear
What the world needs
Isn't so clear

Living Spirit
Loosing Life

What the world needs
Is a way to heal

19

Curse of Death

Black eyes and blue skies
A child cries a mother dies
Red eyes and blood flies
A hero dies a villain sigh

Humans strive the world dies
The world dies humanity cries
Animals die the world cries
Humans kill animals heal

A soul flies a body returns
Memories lost only to be recovered
The body dies Gaia welcomes the soul
Gaia heals and then lets you go

The rain falls the sun shines
A man cries a woman says bye
A gift is lost a curse is found
The gift of life the curse of death

Consequences

Hunted since the day I was born
By an order dark and forlorn
My future in the hands of fate
And fueled by the men of hate

Pictures of our future and past
Always fade and never last
Songs we have written poems we have felt
Is all we have had but never been dealt

Feelings locked deep in our soul
Sit and simmer and take a toll
Fibs and lies help us live
But teach mankind not to give

My soul from day one
Has been hidden from the sun
Marked by the hands of fate
To never reach the golden gate

My immortality taken away
For a toll that I must pay
For something I did in the past
The pain never fades but long lasts

Six Feet Under

Three feet under
Plus, three feet more
Equals a grave
Dug for the poor

No feet under
Cement block floors
A rich mans' tomb
With closable doors

An unmarked grave
Dug in the night
Equals a poplars grave
With no mark in sight

Six feet under
Is good for most
No one to judge them
No one to boast

A shallow grave
Dug for a pet
Easy to dig up
Easy to forget

A cement building
Called a tomb
Built for Egyptians
With plenty of room

A small coffin
Put in the ground
With you or someone in it
And no one around

Stuck in a hole
Six feet in the ground
Never going to leave
Never making a sound

Hang, Burn and Bleed

Burn to death
You fucken Witch
Die like
 a Bloody Bitch
Hang, Burn and Bleed

Never let them
See you cry
As they sit
And watch you die
Hang, Burn and Bleed

You know you will go on
As I sit and sing this song
Do not fear do not cry
For we never really die
Hang, Burn and Bleed

You know the story now
And you don't know how
As you wonder what to do
Something calls and becomes you

Hang, Burn and Bleed

The pain is cutting like a knife
Yet you do not know your strife
For a friend is helping you
Do what you know you must do
Hang, Burn and Bleed

Millions of eyes are watching you
Some know what you can do
They want to see you die in pain
Make you know lives lived in vain
Hang, Burn and Bleed

As you see your life pass by
You finally close your eyes and die
The earth withers in their eye
Everyone lets out a surprised cry
Hang, Burn and Bleed

The world is gone forever now
Someone killed it with a pow
Threefold times threefold be
Killed the world with the power of three
Hang, Burn and Bleed

The earth is the devils now
For he has slaughtered Gabriel
The armies must go on

So, I sing this marching song
Hang, Burn and Bleed

It is the battle of the era
The outcome depends on Sierra
For she has the hidden key
And so, it must be
Hang, Burn and Bleed

Everything will be set free
From this earth you will see
Soon everyone will die like me
And so mote it be
Hang, Burn and Bleed

I am hanging in the shadows
I am burning in the ashes
I am Bleeding out my soul
And you will die like me
Hang, Burn and Bleed

Devine family

Touched by the hands of the Devil
Hands washed in sin
Hands washed in blood
Hands washed in tears

Touched by the hands of God
Hands washed in faith
Hands washed in love
Hands washed in sin

Touched by the hands of Mother Earth
Hands washed in truth
Hands washed in compassion
Hands washed in love

Touched by the hands of Father Sky
Hands washed in understanding
Hands washed in wonder
Hands washed in light

Touched by the hands of Grandmother moon
Hands washed in wishes
Hands washed in dreams
Hands washed in night

Touched by the hands of Grandfather Sun
Hands washed in warmth
Hands washed in hope
Hands washed in sight

Past and Present

Back when the world was new
And the sky was a healthy blue
Every creature lived as one
Under the healthy moon and sun

Back when water was clear
And no one had to live in fear
Every creature had a healthy life
And not have to life in rife

Back when people were new
There were very few
They lived as one on this earth
Respecting every new birth

Back when there was no greed
And every creature on earth was free
There was a perfect balance
Between everything that existed

Now the world is old
No one listens to the stories told
The old ways lost in the sand
And balance gone like a helping hand

Now the water is murky and has dead features
Pollution is killing the world and its creatures
No one cares to change our ways
And because of that everyone pays

Scared

Have you ever been scared
To look in the mirror
Scared of what you would find
Or something left behind

Have you ever been
Scared to look in a dark room
Scared of what you would see
Something that should not be there
Or something more unexpected

Have you ever been
Scared to be alive
Scared of what could happen
Scared of what you would lose
And how you could manage to survive

Have you ever been
Scared to look within yourself
Scared of who you are
Or what might be hidden
Or something your soul left behind

The time has come

The time has come
To follow the flow
Follow the flow

The time has come
For me to let go
Me to let go

The time has come
To say good-bye
Say Good-bye

The time has come
For you to cry
You to cry

The time has come
For me to die
Me to die

The Pain of Words

Words used against me
To harm or upset me
Now bottled and jarred
In the recesses of my soul
One day when it overflows
And the lid no longer fits
I will finally have the courage
To end the pain and anger
I have felt everyday of my life

Words of pain and anger
Used as ammo to put me down
Are used to load the gun
That is inside my mind
Waiting for the pull of the trigger
To blow everything I know away
To a place of rest and peace
Away from a world of pain and judgement

You don't know

You see but you don't care
You feel but you don't show
You hurt but you won't heal
You're dying but you don't know
You're dying but you don't know

You hear but your unwise
You care but care too much
Your pain is shared with all
You're dying but you don't know
You're dying but you don't know

You work but work to hard
You think but think to much
You try but can't succeed
You're dying and you don't know
You're dying and you don't know

Your fast but should slow down
You're here but stuck back there
Your loved but only see hate
You're dying but you don't know
You're dying but you don't know

Your pain is killing you inside

Your strong but it's your demise
You're here but sins in your eyes
You're dying and now you know
You're dying and now you know

My Path

Straight and narrow
Is the path I walk
The path chosen for me
The path that leads me no where

Circle after circle
Is the path I run
The path chosen for me
Leads me back to where it begun

Straight and narrow
Is the path I walk
The path I follow
And am always chasing

Circle after circle
Is the path I run
The path I follow
And always ends where it begun

Straight and narrow
Is the path I walk
Until I create a trail
Along with my own destiny